A GREAT EXPLORERS BOOK

A Long -AND- Uncertain Journey

The 27,000-Mile Voyage of Vasco da Gama

MIKAYA PRESS

NEW YORK

Editor: Stuart Waldman
Design: Lesley Ehlers Design

Library of Congress Cataloging-in-publication Data

Goodman, Joan E.
A long and uncertain journey : the 27,000 mile voyage of Vasco da Gama/ by Joan
Elizabeth Goodman; illustrated by Tom McNeely.
p.cm.—(A great explorers book)
ISBN 0-9650493-7-X (hc)
1. Gama, Vasco da, 1469-1524—Journeys—Juvenile literature. 2.
Explorers—Portugal—Biography—Juvenile literature. 3. Discoveries in
geography—Portuguese—Juvenile literature. 1. McNeely, Tom 11. Title. 111. Series.

G286.G2 G63 2001
910'92—dcl
[B]   00-063795

Printed in China

A LONG -AND- UNCERTAIN JOURNEY

The 27,000-Mile Voyage of Vasco da Gama

By Joan Elizabeth Goodman

Illustrated by Tom McNeely

MIKAYA PRESS

NEW YORK

The people considered us already lost
On so long and uncertain a journey,
The women with piteous wailing,
The men with agonizing sighs...

From The Lusíads, *a 16th-century epic poem
about the voyage of Vasco da Gama.*

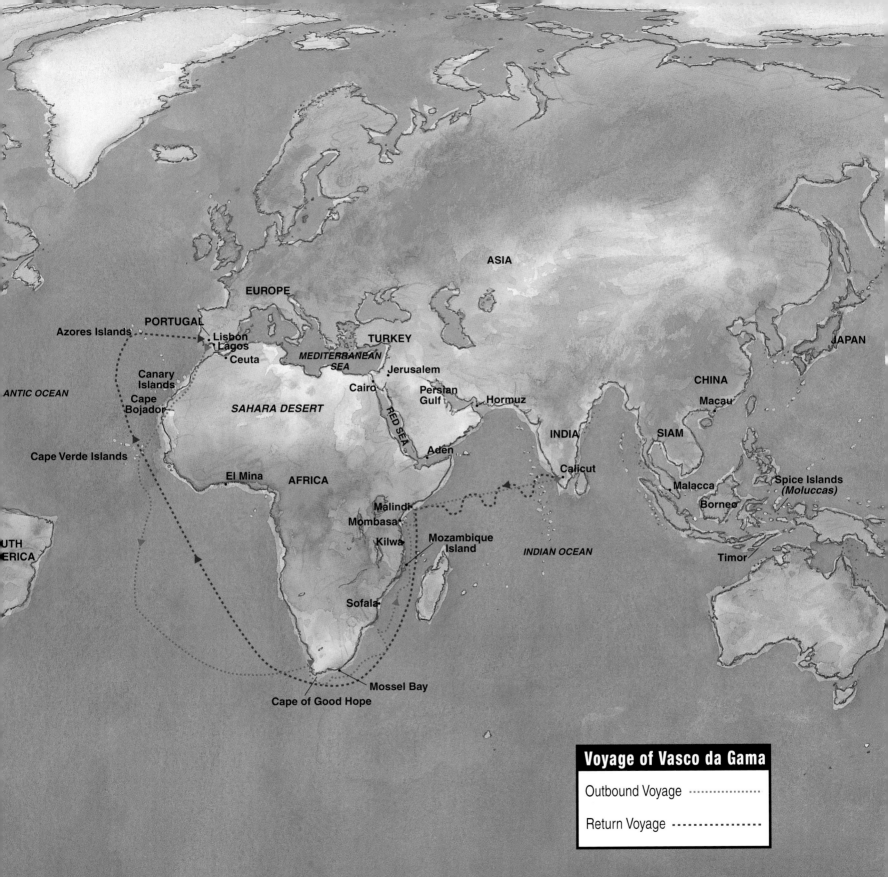

ASIA

EUROPE

PORTUGAL

Azores Islands

ATLANTIC OCEAN

Lisbon
Lagos
Ceuta

Canary
Islands

Cape
Bojador

Cape Verde Islands

El Mina

AFRICA

SAHARA DESERT

MEDITERRANEAN
SEA

TURKEY

Jerusalem

Cairo

RED SEA

Persian
Gulf

Aden

Hormuz

INDIA

JAPAN

CHINA

Macau

SIAM

Calicut

Malacca

Borneo

Spice Islands
(Moluccas)

Malindi

Mombasa

Kilwa

Mozambique
Island

INDIAN OCEAN

Timor

SOUTH
AMERICA

Sofala

Mossel Bay

Cape of Good Hope

Voyage of Vasco da Gama

Outbound Voyage ·············

Return Voyage ------------

The Voyage of Vasco da Gama

Keep the other side of this page open.
You can read about Vasco da Gama's
travels and follow them on the map
at the same time.

ver five hundred years ago, King Manuel of Portugal sent four ships, commanded by Vasco da Gama, to find the sea route to India and bring back the most valuable commodities of the Middle Ages—spices. When he returned to Lisbon in 1499 after two years of voyaging, da Gama brought back only two of the ships and one-third of his men. Furthermore, his ships carried mere handfuls of the precious spices they'd been sent to find.

But the king did not throw da Gama into the dungeons. Instead, King Manuel named him Admiral of the Indian Ocean.

Vasco da Gama was the first to sail from Europe around the vast continent of Africa, across the treacherous Indian Ocean, to India and the riches of the Orient. His journey of some 27,000 miles, nearly four times the distance Columbus sailed in 1492, was the culmination of seventy years and hundreds of Portuguese voyages of exploration. Because of Vasco da Gama, it no longer mattered that Portugal was a poor sliver of land with few natural resources. She could now reach out and claim half of the globe as her own!

Portugal's exploration of the world grew out of religious wars, called the Crusades, that started in the 11th century. European Christians poured across the Mediterranean Sea to fight Moslem Arabs for lands sacred to them both, especially the city of Jerusalem. The slaughter on both sides was staggering and continued for centuries.

In 1415, twenty-one year-old Prince Henry of Portugal led a successful assault on Ceuta, a wealthy Moslem city in North Africa. Ceuta's prosperity was based on its trade with the Orient.

Stretching from North Africa to the Red Sea and the Persian Gulf, the Moslem world was ideally located to control valuable trade routes. Moslem ships and caravans regularly went to India, China, and the Spice Islands to buy silks, fine porcelain, gems, and the spices that made medieval foods edible. These luxuries were sold in Europe at a thousand times their original cost. Camel caravans went south of the Sahara to trade for African gold and rare ivory. When Prince Henry saw these riches in the marketplace of Ceuta, he conceived of a new way to combat Moslems.

Prince Henry believed that Portugal's location just north of the African continent, and her able sailors and shipbuilders, gave her advantages equal to those of the Moslems. His plan was to establish new trade routes by sending Portuguese ships down the coast of Africa, and eventually around it to the Orient. He would build a trading empire to rival that of the Moslem enemy, and, in the process, he would make Portugal very rich.

It was a tremendous undertaking. Europeans had no knowledge of the African coast. They didn't know how long it was, where it ended, if it ended, or if a navigable route to India existed. Although Portuguese mariners were among the most skilled in the world, navigating the coast of Africa would prove difficult and deadly. Portugal's war may have been with the Moslems, but her first battles were against the sea.

A 16th-century spice merchant weighing nutmeg as if it were gold.

From the Journal of a witness at the slave market at Lagos, Portugal

1441

Some kept their heads low and their faces bathed in tears; others stood groaning, looking up at the height of heaven; others struck their faces with the palms of their hands, throwing themselves in full length upon the ground....
As soon as they had placed them in one part, the sons, seeing their fathers in another, rushed over to them; the mothers clasped their children and threw themselves on the ground.

The greatest obstacle that Prince Henry's mariners faced was fear. In the early fifteenth century, the size and nature of the world was still a great mystery. The first sailors to venture south along the African coast were sure that they would run into boiling seas and gigantic, ship-devouring monsters. Cape Bojador, only a few hundred miles from Portugal, was the main stumbling block. It was surrounded by treacherous currents and deadly reefs; the water actually looked like it was boiling. Sailors were convinced that beyond Bojador lay death.

In 1434, after years and dozens of voyages by others, Gil Eanes, one of Prince Henry's captains, summoned up the courage to push beyond Bojador. He found there were no monsters and that the seas could be navigated. Eanes had opened the sea road to Africa.

Prince Henry sent ship after ship farther and farther south. Seven years after Eanes's voyage a ship returned with cargo that would bring Portugal tremendous wealth. The hold carried neither gold nor ivory, but African people.

In 1441, Europe's first slave market was held at Lagos, Portugal. Two hundred Africans were sold. Children were torn from their mothers' arms, brother separated from brother, and friend from friend. Yet the enterprise was deemed good and holy because these pagan Africans would be converted to Christianity. Prince Henry himself watched it all with pleasure and satisfaction.

Saved souls also yielded an earthly reward. Slavery was enormously profitable. Soon thousands of people were taken every year from Africa to be sold at high prices in Europe. The profits filled the king's coffers and helped finance Portugal's later explorations, including the voyage of Vasco da Gama.

By the time Prince Henry died in 1460, his mariners had explored nearly 1500 miles, a third of the African coastline. Under the leadership of King João II, Portugal was ready for the next step: going around the southernmost part of Africa and heading east to the Orient.

Currents and winds along the coast made it difficult to navigate. In 1488, Bartolomeu Dias, after struggling down the coast, ran into even greater storms as he approached the tip of Africa. In desperation, Dias steered his ship into the open Atlantic, away from the turbulence. There, the winds blew him past the tip. His voyage proved that it was possible to sail around Africa.

Meanwhile, another explorer, Pero da Covilhã, traveled overland to learn as much as he could about the mysterious Indian Ocean to the east of Africa. His journey took him through Europe and across the Mediterranean Sea to Cairo. There, disguised as a Moslem merchant, Covilhã joined a caravan to Aden, where the Red Sea meets the Indian Ocean. He boarded a ship bound for the port of Calicut on the west coast of India. Indian jewels, pepper and ginger, cinnamon and cloves from the Spice Islands, silk and porcelain from China, and gold and ivory from Africa were traded in the markets of Calicut. It was the great

Prince Henry became known as Henry the Navigator because of his leadership of Portugal's explorations of the world.

meeting place of eastern and western trade routes and the heart of the Moslem trading empire.

The voyage of Dias had given Portugal a nearly complete picture of the outline of Africa. The journey of Covilhã showed what lay beyond. Finally, after more than seventy years, the stage was set for the fulfillment of Prince Henry's dream.

riests and crimson-robed bishops chanting prayers led the grand procession of nobles in satins and lace, ships' captains and seamen in their finest, through the packed streets to Lisbon's harbor. The mariners boarded the ships with the blessings of the priests. Cannons thundered. The ships weighed anchor, their sails took the wind, and they sailed down the Tagus River to the sea. The air was electric with excitement as Portugal embarked on her great adventure.

But not all were cheering. This voyage would be far longer, and more dangerous, than any before. The wrenching cries of wives and mothers, many saying good-bye to their men forever, competed with the triumphal blare of trumpets and the booming drums.

It was July 8, 1497. Vasco da Gama was setting out on the greatest voyage ever attempted. Little information about him exists before this date. He grew up in a small coastal town where his father had been given an estate as reward for his service in fighting the Moslems. He studied mathematics and navigation. Serving on the king's ships, he was noted for his skill as a pilot and for capturing an enemy ship. He was a capable captain, a fighting man, and a fervent enemy of Moslems—all these were good reasons to choose da Gama as a leader. But there must have been another, even more compelling reason for King Manuel to name him captain-major, commander of the fleet. A man of steely resolve was needed to complete a journey of such magnitude. The captain-major would have to keep the fleet going and not be dissuaded by unwilling crews. He would have to remain firm no matter the danger. Something about Vasco da Gama must have convinced his king that he could succeed.

Da Gama commanded four ships. His flagship, the *São Gabriel*, and the *São Raphael*, captained by his brother Paulo da Gama, were *nãos*. These broader, heavier ships were especially designed for this voyage. With them went the smaller *Berrio* and a supply ship. All together they carried about 170 men.

The ships headed south to the Cape Verde Islands off the African coast. From there da Gama set a new course. All previous voyages had continued directly south and hugged the coast. The age-old fear of the open sea kept the ships following the shoreline despite treacherous currents and opposing winds. It had taken Dias six months to round the Cape of Good Hope following this route. Da Gama needed a faster sea road. He may have heard tales of favorable winds to be found in the western Atlantic. He may have been influenced by Dias's course around the Cape. Whatever his reasons, he headed the ships away from the African coast into the southwest Atlantic. It was a brilliant stroke.

The Journal of the Voyage of Vasco da Gama

July 8, 1497

In the name of God. Amen!
In the year 1497, King Dom Manuel, the first of that name in Portugal, dispatched four vessels to make discoveries and go in search of spices. Vasco da Gama was the captain-major of these vessels....
May God our Lord permit us to accomplish this voyage in his service. Amen!

Unlike Dias, who sailed just a few miles off the coast, da Gama sailed thousands of miles into the Atlantic. At one point, he was closer to South America than to Africa. No doubt his crews were terrified. For over three months, the endless sea surrounded the small fleet. The Atlantic was a continuous heaving and swelling. Watery valleys grew to watery mountains, and mountains melted into valleys, yet all remained sea.

Storms raged. Lightning set the sky afire, and thunder roared. Each crashing wave was a reminder of the frailty of the wooden vessels that stood between the men and death. At times the night was absolutely black, and the ships floated in a fearsome emptiness. Below the equator the constellations of the northern hemisphere were no longer visible. The North Star, Orion, and the Great Bear that the sailors had always depended on were gone. The strange southern constellations brought little comfort.

Mariners saw sights as frightening as any nightmare. A quavering blue flame, actually a charge of electricity caused by storms, called St. Elmo's fire, traveled the ships' mastheads and spars. Whirling winds sucked the ocean up into a giant column of water. As the wind diminished, a deluge of salt rain poured down on the helpless ships. Each passing day depleted food and water supplies, and what remained became nearly too putrid to eat or drink. Ships' biscuits were more worm than biscuit. Water was so foul the sailors drank it through their handkerchiefs to filter off the scum. Only a firm and respected commander could have kept his men sailing into the unknown. Grumbling could have quickly turn to mutiny, as had happened on many earlier voyages. But da Gama tolerated neither disobedience, nor dissent.

On November 4, after 4500 miles and 96 days on the open sea, land was sighted. His gamble had paid off. They'd come to the southern tip of Africa in half the time it had taken Dias. The four ships drew near to each other. The men put on their gala clothes and dressed the ships with flags and pennants. They saluted their captain-major, firing their cannons. Vasco da Gama had brought them through the terrifying seas and safely back to land.

Da Gama and his men began the second stage of their journey. Now, after the perilous and unpredictable sea, they faced an even greater challenge in their encounters with the peoples of Africa.

How strange and frightening these unwashed, hairy, overdressed Portuguese must have looked to the Hottentots, the tribe of that region. Certainly as strange as the small, nearly naked, brown-skinned African herders looked to the Portuguese. Only the dogs were familiar, barking just as they did in Portugal.

Neither Portuguese nor Hottentot could understand the other's language. Da Gama had brought translators who spoke Arabic and the language of central West Africa. But that didn't help here, in the remotest part of the world. Words, gestures, sounds could easily be misunderstood. It's not surprising that the encounters were fraught with tension, as the mood could shift in the blink of an eye.

At times the chasm of difference was bridged by shared delight. At Mossel Bay, the Hottentots were given trinkets, round bells, and red caps from the ships' stores. A week later, some two hundred of them came, bringing oxen, sheep, and cows. They began to play on flutes and danced. Vasco da Gama ordered trumpets to be sounded. The captain-major and his men all joined in the dance.

Later though, these same joyful dancers refused to let da Gama's ships replenish their supplies of water. And, as the ships were leaving Mossel Bay, the Hottentots came forward and demolished the stone pillar and wooden cross da Gama's men had erected the day before. The Africans didn't need to understand Portuguese to know that foreigners planting a marker on their land meant trouble.

The Journal of the Voyage of Vasco da Gama

December 2, 1497

They forthwith began to play on four or five flutes, some prouducing high notes and others low ones, thus making a pretty harmony for negroes who are not expected to be musicians. The captain-major then ordered the trumpets to be sounded, and we danced, and the captain-major did likewise.

Portuguese explorers carried with them stone pillars, called *padrões*, to mark new lands as belonging to Portugal.

By Christmas the ships, now on the east coast of Africa, had gone over 200 miles beyond the farthest point of Dias's voyage. They were in completely uncharted waters, and constantly in danger of reefs that could rip the belly of a wooden ship. The empty supply ship, having served its purpose, was burned. The casks of drinking water were nearly empty. Salt-preserved food had to be cooked in briny seawater. Their situation was desperate.

On January 11, da Gama and his men found a warm reception with people of the Bantu tribe. The chief offered them whatever was needed. For five days the ships took on fresh water and traded with the tall, black-skinned natives. A favoring wind propelled them up the coast to a low, marshy country where grew many tall fruit trees. Here da Gama stayed for thirty-two days. The ships needed repairs and more water. The men were exhausted. Many were sick with scurvy, a deadly disease caused by lack of fresh fruits and vegetables in their diets. Some men had already died, and many more would.

Yet, this was a hopeful place. Here were the first signs that they were nearing the Orient. The people wore cloth woven in India. They spoke of trading ships and far-off lands.

The Journal of the Voyage of Vasco da Gama

January 28, 1498

Two gentlemen of the country came to see us. They were very haughty and valued nothing which we gave them. One of them wore a cap with a fringe embroidered of silk, and the other a cap of green satin....
These tokens gladdened our hearts for it appeared as if we were really approaching the place of our desires.

On February 24, da Gama set sail, now confident that he was drawing nearer to his goal. On March 2, they arrived at Mozambique Island. Whitewashed houses and gleaming mosques surrounded a bustling harbor. This was completely different from the villages of the Bantu and Hottentots.

Mozambique Island was populated by wealthy merchants. Centuries before a Moslem sect had left Arabia and come to the East African coast where they'd established independent trading cities. Arabs and Bantus had intermarried, and the people of Mozambique Island were various shades of beige, brown, and black, but all were faithful Moslems. Their ships, called *dhows*, brought gems, spices, and fine porcelain from the East to trade for the goods of Africa.

For the first time the Portuguese had the wealth of the Orient right before their eyes. They could smell the heady spices, touch the gleaming gems. And this was only a sample of what was to come. Da Gama was told that precious stones, pearls, and spices were so plentiful in India that they could be scooped up in baskets. He hired two Moslem pilots to guide him across the Indian Ocean to the land of riches.

Initially the people of Mozambique, mistaking the Portuguese for Moslem traders from Turkey, gave them a warm welcome. That welcome turned sour when the sultan of Mozambique and an entourage of elegantly dressed nobles came to pay their respects. Da Gama offered the sultan caps and coral beads as a gift. The cheap trinkets that had charmed the Hottentots of south Africa only insulted the worldly sultan. Relations deteriorated even further when it became clear to the sultan that he was dealing with the Christian enemy. Hospitality ceased. When the mariners tried to fill their casks with fresh water, they met with resistance and armed threats. Da Gama was not a man to take this lightly. He fired his cannons on the town, killing at least three men. Before sailing north da Gama went out of his way to capture and loot a number of small merchant vessels, taking several Moslems prisoner.

The Moslem pilots assured da Gama that in Mombasa, the city they were approaching, they would find a welcoming Christian community. Perhaps da Gama should have been suspicious, but they were telling him something he wanted to hear. All along da Gama had hoped that he would find Prester John, the legendary ruler of a Christian kingdom somewhere in Africa or Asia. The story of Prester John persisted throughout the Middle Ages, although no traveler or merchant ever found the king or his country. Part of da Gama's mission was to locate Prester John and win him as an ally for Portugal against the Moslems.

The Moslem king of Mombasa sent oranges, sheep, and a ring as a sign of his welcome. His representatives, who said they were Christian, told tales of Christian cities and the nearby kingdom of Prester John. It was just as da Gama had hoped, and he prepared to enter the port—and a waiting trap!

The Journal of the Voyage of Vasco da Gama

April 7, 1498

The pilots who had come with us told us there resided both Moslems and Christians in this city; that these latter lived apart under their own lords, and that on our arrival they would receive us with much honor and take us into their houses.

As da Gama dropped anchor, the Moslem pilots leapt overboard. The captain-major finally became suspicious. He had two of the Moslem prisoners tortured with boiling oil dripped on their skin. They revealed that the pilots were in on a plot against the Portuguese. The king of Mombasa, who had been warned about da Gama by the sultan of Mozambique, planned to attack the ships once they entered the enclosed port. Da Gama and his men sailed away unscathed, but still without enough supplies to reach India or a pilot to guide them.

On April 15, 1498, Easter Sunday, the Portuguese had a special reason to rejoice: they'd come to Malindi, a truly welcoming port. The king, although a Moslem, was the enemy of the rulers of Mozambique and Mombasa. He was eager to form an alliance against them, even with Christians. He offered da Gama all that was needed of food and fresh water. Most important, Malindi provided the Portuguese with a skilled and trustworthy pilot to guide them to India.

The Portuguese left Malindi on April 24. The pilot threaded the maze of atolls and reefs along the East African coast. Five days later the ships crossed the equator. Once again the crew saw familiar skies with the same stars that shone over Portugal. What a welcome sight for the homesick mariners!

The ships headed across the Indian Ocean toward the great trading city of Calicut. Catching the beginning of the spring monsoon, the seasonal storm that blew eastward, they arrived at their destination three weeks later on May 20, 1498.

The Journal of the Voyage of Vasco da Gama

April 18, 1498

The King [of Malindi] wore a robe of damask trimmed with green satin and a rich cap. He was seated on two cushioned chairs of bronze beneath a round sunshade of crimson satin attached to a pole.... There were two trumpets of ivory richly carved and the size of a man, which were blown from holes in the side and made sweet harmony.

India!

The arrival of the three Portuguese ships made quite an impression. They were vastly different from the Arab merchants' *dhows* that plied the Indian Ocean. The much larger *nãos* bristled with cannons and caught the attention of the Zamorin, the Hindu ruler of Calicut. He sent a suitable escort to bring the foreign captain to his palace.

Vasco da Gama rode high above the crowds on a palanquin borne by six strong men. The two hundred Indian soldiers with swords drawn that surrounded the Portuguese were necessary to part the crowds that had come to gape at the strangers from Europe. One of the noble lords attending da Gama brought drummers, pipers, and trumpeters. Da Gama was pleased: this was a proper welcome for the emissary of the king of Portugal!

Still after what had happened in Africa, the captain-major remained on his guard. He gave orders for his ships to leave him and sail immediately for home if anything went wrong. No matter what happened, King Manuel must know that they'd succeeded in reaching India.

The procession stopped at a Hindu temple where the Portuguese saw images of gods and goddesses. The Portuguese knew that these definitely weren't Moslem. Having no knowledge of Hinduism, they assumed the images were Christian. All bowed down in homage to one they thought was the Virgin Mary. (They must have wondered at the paintings and statues of 'saints,' some of whom had fangs and several arms.) The willingness of the Portuguese to believe that this temple was a cathedral shows how eager they were to find a Christian ally in Asia.

At the palace of the great Zamorin, a throng of nobles came out to meet the captain-major and escort him into an interior court. There the Zamorin reclined on a couch of velvet with cushions and coverings of the finest weave of cotton. Above him was a canopy elaborately embroidered in gold. He was naked to the waist, his long black hair twined with pearls the size of grapes. Emeralds and rubies hung from golden chains around his neck.

The Zamorin ordered water for his guests to wash, and fruits to refresh them. When Vasco da Gama was presented, he said that he was an ambassador from the king of Portugal.

Da Gama proved himself a worthy ambassador, if not entirely honest. He gained the Zamorin's interest by describing Manuel, King of Portugal, as the ruler of many lands and vastly wealthy. Da Gama emphasized the desirability of an alliance between Portugal and India. This approach must have appealed to the Zamorin, who said that he would send ambassadors to Portugal and that he wished to be a friend and brother to King Manuel. Even though India had trade agreements established centuries before with the Moslems, the Zamorin could appreciate having a new and wealthy ally in the West.

The following day da Gama laid out the gifts he intended for the ruler of Calicut: twelve pieces of striped cloth, four scarlet hoods, six hats, four strings of coral, six hand basins, a case of sugar, two casks each of oil and honey.

It seems impossible that Vasco da Gama would dare to offer the Indian ruler these trifles, especially after he'd seen the luxury of the palace. If the Sultan of Mozambique had scoffed at such gifts, how could da Gama think that they would be acceptable to the Zamorin?

It isn't known why da Gama was so ill-prepared, but sending the ships to India with nothing more to offer than cloth, beads, and trinkets was a fatal mistake. The Moslem advisors to the Zamorin scoffed at the Portuguese presents, saying that "the poorest merchant from Mecca or any other part of India gave more." If da Gama wished to give a present, it should be gold.

The paltry gifts had given the Moslem merchants an opening to turn the Zamorin against the Portuguese. They realized that if the Portuguese got a foothold in Calicut, their trade was in jeopardy. And knowing well the ferocity of Christian crusaders, they feared for their lives as well.

The Journal of the Voyage of Vasco da Gama

June 24, 1498

All on board ship went on land by twos and threes, taking with them bracelets, clothes, new shirts, and other articles, which they desired to sell.... And just as we sold shirts cheaply, we sold other things in order to take some things away from this country....

Although granted another meeting, da Gama was kept waiting in an antechamber for several hours. In a fit of temper, he burst into the court. Unruffled, the Zamorin asked him, "Why, if his was such a rich country, did he come empty-handed?" Da Gama tried to explain that his was purely a voyage of discovery.

"Did you hope to discover stones or men?" asked the Zamorin, implying that men required the courtesy of gifts.

Despite the Zamorin's disdain, da Gama was allowed to unload his cargo and try to sell it. The Portuguese wheat, cloth, iron, and bronze were as little valued as the trinkets. No one would buy any of it. Certainly the Moslems wouldn't touch the Portuguese wares, and spat on the ground whenever the mariners passed.

Da Gama sent his crews ashore to sell whatever they could, just to get something from India to show their king. The men traded their own possessions and got a few grains of spice and chips of gemstones.

He sent Diogo Dias, one of his officers, to the Zamorin with amber, coral beads, and "other things." They probably weren't any more impressive than his first attempted gifts. Dias begged for quantities of clove, cinnamon, and other spices for the king of Portugal.

The Zamorin ignored the request.

It was time for da Gama and his men to return home. They set sail on October 5, but the monsoon winds that had carried them so swiftly to Calicut were now dead against them. Instead of the twenty-seven days it took to reach Calicut, the Portuguese were nearly three months in returning to East Africa.

During that time nearly all the crew suffered from scurvy. Their gums, swollen with foul, black blood, engulfed their teeth. The men couldn't eat; they could barely drink. Their legs and arms swelled until they could not move. And then they died. Thirty men died, added to the thirty, or more, who'd already died on the journey. Only seven or eight men were well enough to navigate each ship, and they were ill, too. Had this gone on any longer, none of the Portuguese would have returned home, and their accomplishments would have been lost in the waves.

They were saved by a sudden brisk tail wind, which brought them within sight of land. And all of those who were able celebrated. On January 7, they returned to the friendly haven of Malindi. The Portuguese were again received warmly by the king, who sent sheep, oranges, and other fruit. Many of the sick were too far gone to be saved and perished.

Paulo da Gama was now seriously ill with tuberculosis. He could no longer act as captain, and too few men were left to sail all three ships. On January 11, they anchored just past Mombasa, and set fire to the *São Raphael*.

After that the journey proceeded quickly. They passed close by the East African coast but carefully avoided Mozambique Island. On March 20, they rounded the Cape of Good Hope. The wind, now at their backs, carried them swiftly up the West African coast. Nearing their destination, the *Berrio* and the *São Gabriel* were separated in a storm. The *Berrio* arrived safely in Lisbon on July 10, 1499. Vasco da Gama took Paulo to the island of Terceira in the Azores, where he hoped the healthy air would save him. Paulo died the day after they landed.

Remaining on Terceira, mourning his brother, da Gama didn't return to Lisbon until August 29. On September 8, he was formally received by his grateful king, his long journey ended.

Vasco da Gama's daring leap into the unknown waters of the south Atlantic had opened the definitive sea route from Europe around Africa to India. His voyage gave the Portuguese an understanding of how the Moslems managed trade in Africa and Asia, and that they meant to keep that trade for themselves. Portugal could neither negotiate nor buy her way in. However, da Gama's voyage also showed that Portugal's ships and weapons were unmatched in the Indian Ocean. Portugal could blast her way in.

Eighteen months after da Gama's return, King Manuel sent a fleet of thirteen armed vessels and 1,200 men led by Pedro Álvares Cabral to India. The Zamorin got the message. Trade was established between Calicut and the Portuguese, but the Moslems opposed the agreement. They incited riots in which fifty Portuguese were killed. Cabral retaliated and subdued the Moslems—at least temporarily.

Da Gama returned to the East in 1502 heading an armada of twenty ships. He meant to completely destroy Moslem commerce. Any hint of opposition was met with savage cruelty. When the Zamorin refused to banish Calicut's Moslems, da Gama captured a boat full of Hindus. He hanged the prisoners from his masts, and hacked them to pieces. He sent the bloody remains back to the Zamorin. Then, turning his cannons on Calicut, he watched its wooden houses burn.

Hundreds of Moslem and Hindu innocents perished.

Da Gama returned to Lisbon in 1503. This time his ships were full to bursting with spices. The Moslem merchants were defeated. For centuries trade in the Indian Ocean had been arranged by treaty and negotiation. The Portuguese had taken it by force. Indian and African trade had been changed forever. And so had the world.

Vasco da Gama made one last trip to the Orient when he was made Viceroy of Portuguese India. He only ruled for eight months before falling sick and dying on Christmas Eve, 1524. By then Portugal had established fortresses along the East African coast at Mozambique, Kilwa, and Sofala. She had conquered Hormuz, in the Arabian Gulf, and the most important trading city in the East Indies, Malacca. The Portuguese pushed on to the Spice Islands (Moluccas), Borneo, and Timor. Meanwhile trade had begun with Japan and Siam and, in 1557, a trading base was established in Macau, a tiny island off mainland China.

Gaining her far-flung empire was one thing; keeping it was something else. The Portuguese were thousands of miles from home, and surrounded by enemies. Never able to attract, nor keep, enough men to defend her fortresses and trade, Portugal lost her empire nearly as quickly as it was won.

It wasn't just the Moslems and Africans that threatened Portugal. Her European neighbors grew greedy for Portugal's possessions. It began with raiding French and Dutch pirates. Soon wealthy Dutch merchants built ships as fast, strong, and well-armed as the Portuguese nãos. In 1605, the Dutch captured the Portuguese bases in the Spice Islands. In 1637, they took the West African fortress of El Mina. In 1641, they won Malacca, and by 1663 they were gaining control in India.

The Portuguese Empire fell like a house of cards.

In 1570, Luís Vaz de Camões wrote The Lusíads, an epic poem glorying in the exploits of Vasco da Gama, and comparing his accomplishments to those of the ancient Greek hero, Odysseus. Camões knew well of what he wrote. His own adventures had taken him throughout the Portuguese Empire. He had experienced shipwreck, pirates, and the endless and terrifying ocean voyages. He saw firsthand the splendor and decay beginning to beset the Empire.

Although The Lusíads celebrated da Gama's achievement, Camões knew what it would eventually cost Portugal. When he described Vasco da Gama's departure on his first voyage, he introduced an old man who steps out of the crowd, silencing the cheers and fanfare. The old man denounces the quest for India, predicting that it will lead to the downfall of Portugal.

> To what new catastrophes do you plan
> To drag this kingdom and these people?...
> You ignore the enemy at the gate
> In search of another so far away.....

Sorrowing for the future, he curses, "the man who first put dry wood in the waves with a sail."

TIMELINE

1415 Portugal conquers Ceuta.

1434 Gil Eanes sails past Cape Bojador

1441 African slaves are sold at Europe's first slave market.

1460 Prince Henry the Navigator dies.

1487 Pero da Covilhã leaves for India.

1488 Bartolomeu Dias rounds Africa.

1497 Vasco da Gama departs Lisbon.

1498 Da Gama reaches Calicut.

1500 Pedro Álvares Cabral departs India.

1502 Da Gama's second voyage to India.

1505 Portugal builds forts in Kilwa and Sofala.

1511 Portugal captures Malacca.

1512 Portugal establishes trading stations in the Spice Islands.

1515 Portugal captures Hormuz.

1516 Portugal lands in Timor.

1524 Vasco da Gama dies.

1543 Portugal lands in Japan.

1557 Portugal obtains Macau.

1570 Camões writes *The Lusíads*.

1605 Portugal loses the Spice Islands.

1622 Portugal loses Hormuz.

1650 Portugal is expelled from Japan.

1663 The Dutch capture Portuguese bases in India.

INDEX

CREDITS

Borromeo/ Art Resource, NY: p. 32

Gianni Dagli Orti/CORBIS: p. 8

Giraudon/ Art Resource, NY: p. 33 (bottom left)

Giraudon/ Art Resource, NY: p. 10

Tom McNeely: pp. 5, 12-13, 16-17, 19, 22-23, 25, 26, 29, 30, 34, 38, 42-43

The Pierpont Morgan Library/ Art Resource, NY: p. 33 (top)

Victoria & Albert Museum, London/ Art Resource, NY: p.33 (bottom right)

AUTHOR'S NOTE

The Journal of Vasco da Gama's voyage
was written by a member of the crew. We
don't know his name, but we're lucky to
have this sailor's rich and vivid portrait of
the journey and its captain-major.

Vasco da Gama wrote his own reports
of the voyage. Unfortunately, these were lost
in the Lisbon earthquake of 1755.